Table of Conte

OneNote for New Users :

Easy and Simple GuideGetting the Most Out Of OneNote

SIMON BEDFORD

READ THIS FIRST

Just to say thank-you for buying my book, I'd like to offer you **FREE access to OurBookClub.co**

I think you will benefit immensely for joining as you will gain fast access to tons of **FREE EXCLUSIVE CONTENT:**

Signup Bonus (Download):

The Prosperity Bundle (three eBooks):

- Top 10 Ideas to attract Money
- Top 10 Ideas to attract Health
- Top 10 ideas to attract Healthy Relationships

In These 3 FREE BOOKS You'll Learn:

How to build wealth easily, manage your life to attract good health,

enhance your current relationships, and attract "The One"

Other Benefits for joining OurBookClub:

- FREE brand new eBooks (from Gardening, Programming, Cookbooks, Spirituality, Fiction, Self-help and more...)

- Be informed of discounted eBooks

- Chance to have a say in what content you would like for us to add to new book editions

- Free Articles & Videos

- Free Access to an active readers community (soon to be launched)

Ready? **Get Access Now**

Introduction

Taking notes is a practice that people have used for a long time. There are numerous occasions where people have to take notes. From classrooms to offices all the way down to social gatherings. People take notes for many different reasons. Some do it to record brainstormed ideas or work processes while others do so to remember important things. There was a point in time when the only way to take notes was by writing things down on a piece of paper.

Today, things have changed. The use of physical notebooksis not the only way people can capture ideas, thoughts or points worth remembering. With the continuous advancement in computer technology, the note taking process has been simplified significantly. With the option of using technology, people no longer have to bring physicalpens and papersalong with them everywhere. Software companies have creatively developed note taking applications that are much easier and fun to use and more efficient in terms of preserving and protecting information captured by note- takers. These applications have also increased the range of things that users can get done with their technology gadgets.OneNote is one application that has replacedthe age-old note taking tools.

But what makes OneNote so handy? It is a virtual notebook that can be used on any gadget that you likely already take with you everywhere. In today's busy world, peoplewill findthemselves having troubleremembering everything.OneNote can be used forthe simplest of lists like groceries and recipes to the more complicated tasks like complex lecture notes. OneNote is a useful tool for all of those things and many more.

OneNote can seem overwhelming at first, but once you get the hang of it, you will find it a very useful and valuable tool for many different reasons. You are able to customize and personalize your notes in a variety of ways. OneNote has really taken notetaking to a whole new electronic level.

OneNote software application will allow you to carry out a range of activities with ease as you enjoy the latest technology. You can, for instance, scribble down ideas, write notes that are loosely structured, make digital notes that you can later on organize and bind.

OneNote application is compatible with most of the mobile devices that are currently in use whether you are using android, iOS or Windows powered mobile phones, you can surely download this application and use it for your needs. Devices with PC style interfaces, for instance, Windows XP and Windows Vista operating systems can also work well with the software.

Other than being a great digital notebook, OneNote can be a very effective information organizer. You do not have to go through the hassle of organizing important information all the time since this software will make things very easy for you. It is the best digital idea processor that you will get to use by far.

Technology is changing old processes for the better. The new programs and hardware are meant to make things much better and easier for their users.OneNote is one of the best applications designed by Microsoft. It has been created with the design and interface in mind in order to provide the kind of help and organization that people expect from such applications these days.

The software can be a bit intimidating for a new userat the beginning, because it has a wide range of features to explore. Its interface is smooth and precise, but without having an idea about what the software can do, it does require some learning and some getting used to.

This guide will be very helpful as you start using OneNote. It will help you learn about the program faster and discover other ways through which you can use the program for your own gain.With the guide, you do not need to worry about how to create new folders, attach files or color-code the different sections you create in notes. This guide offers everything you need to know about using OneNote.

Chapter 1: Understanding OneNote

OneNote is one of the best Microsoft applications available. It is an idea processor, a notebook, and an information organizer. It is ideal to quickly capture meeting notes, brainstorming notes, ideas and thoughts, audio from discussions, video from interviews, diagrams, and so on using the keyboard or the recording capabilities in OneNote. One can also gather clippings from the web, email, miscellaneous materials for projects, files, and pictures. Microsoft has liberated its digital notebook from Office and put it just about everywhere. It can be used on a Mac, IOS, Android, Chrome, and Windows.

In other words, this is an app that helps one who has a very busy schedule to be more organized and to ensure that all their marvelous and intriguing ideas are captured for later reference. It is very normal for human beings to forget, and we tend to forget a lot. More often than not, you get an idea, and since you did not put it down on pen and paper, you try as hard as you can to remember what the idea you had at the time was to no avail. By learning how to use OneNote, those days are as good as behind you. Read on to discover everything you need to know to start creating a paperless life with OneNote.

When it comes to OneNote, you can expect that you will capture, organize and share all of the notes that you will be placing in your notebook. Truly, this innovative software will be the help that you need.

Who Should Use OneNote?

OneNote is best for people with very demanding jobs and

those who mostly attend to multiple meetings during the week, collaborate with others on projects and do a lot of note-taking. It helps to keep the flood of information neat and tidy. All your notes, including pictures and words are searchable inside OneNote, and they are stored in the cloud and immediately accessible via the OneNote apps for any platform, therefore guaranteeing you that the loss of information is nil.

OneNote is most welcomed by the majority of people who hate paper trails. Having a desk full of piles and piles of papers is just unsightly and can also mess with your morale to work considering you have to go through the papers. With, OneNote, one need not worry about that mess as the app is more organized giving you a clear head and leaving you refreshed as you decide on where to start. When your mind is clear, your work becomes a tad easier,and this is why you should learn how to use the OneNote.

Why Use OneNote

When you go shopping for an application, you have in mind what you want the app to help you do. However, in most cases, you will come across numerous apps that can perform the simpler functions that you need to be done. With the wide variety of note taking applications availablein the market today, it is hard to decide which ofthemwill meet your note taking needs best.The truth is, all the apps out there can help you take notes the ordinary way.However, there is much more to taking notes than just typing what you want to capture, and saving it in your device. One of the elements that make OneNote different from another note taking apps is the suite of unique features it offers that add value to the note taking process. These features are discussed in detail later in this guide but here are some of the things that OneNote app enables you to do:

- **Organizelists:**Notes that are taken onOneNote can be shared with other peopleand any changes made by other people in your circle become visible to everyone in the group. This feature decreases chances of forgetting to purchase something you need, or a last minute requirement for a project.
- **Create recipe lists:** In case your recipe book takes a beating due to over-use, you can transfer your recipes to the OneNote. You have the option to organize them based on main food items that you use.
- **Locate favorite newsitems:**You may not realize it yet, but as you browse the internet, and add content to your OneNote, the app allows you to list the content in the order of favorite items. This makes it easy to access them again so you can read them whenever you want. This feature works well for articles and recipes.
- **Make audio /video recordings:** When using the full version of OneNote, you can record audio and video notes to attach to your notes.
- **Convert Images to Text:**This is probably one of the best features that OneNote has to offer. It allows you to take a picture of a page in a book you love,and it will quicklybe converted to text as long as that text is easy to understand.You need not transcribe it one by one.

All these capabilities and much more makeOneNote a valuable and easy to use application.Asyou go through this guide, you will discover manyimportant featuresof OneNote thatmake it the ideal application for note taking.

If you are wondering how other people use OneNote, you will be pleased toknow some of them use it the same way that you wantto.They basically usethe application to take notes about lessons they learn in school, deliberations from a work meetingandcapturerremindersof things theydo not wantto forget. There are people whouse Microsoft OneNote to improve their lives in a significant way.

For instance, Ysgol Bae Baglan, a new school that is set to open in Wales in September 2016, plans touse Microsoft Surface over the next three years to help students become more organized, not only in taking notes but also in sharing notes with other students.

The schoolwants to be able toshow video clips and enable studentsto listento audio clips without duplication.Finding software that was capable of doing that became an easy task the moment the school tried out Microsoft 365equipped with OneNote. This software makesorganizing, sharing and note taking easier.

The school started by testing the effectiveness of Microsoft 365 in various groups and departments. Initial results of these tests were favorable, with most members of the group showcasing their creativity. As time passed by, the teams startedlearning more about the stuff that thissuite of applications allows them to do. These test outcomes informed the school's decision to use OneNote for over all note taking.

Besides the students, there are teachers who use OneNote to connect with their class. For instance, some teachers create shared notebooks so students understand the lessonsbetter. At the same time, the notebooks also contain necessary details on upcoming quizzes and examinations. The use of OneNote is taking note taking to degree whole new level.

How OneNote Is Organized

OneNote is organized by Notebooks, sections, and pages similar to printed, spiral-bound notebook.

- o **Notebooks-** Are the major organization category.
- o **Sections in the current Notebook-** Sections let you organize notes by activities, topic, or people in your life. You start with a few in each notebook.
- o **Pages in the current section-** Create as many note pages in each section as you want or as necessary.

After understanding how OneNote is organized, it is time for you to advance to the next level as you need to learn the basics on how to go about creating your own notebook.

The Design and Basics of OneNote

The great thing about the OneNote is its ability to look similar to the physical notebook. For users who are not quite ready to let go of their notebooks yet but at the same time would like to have the convenience of using an application, the design of this is perfect.

Expect to Have Multiple Notebooks

This is similar to having a lot of subjects in school. You cannot expect that all of the lessons that you have learned in Science will also be in the same notebook wherein you would be placing all of your notes in Math. You need to have separate notebooks so that you will know what to get.

With the OneNote, for each notebook that you have, there will be tabs that are available. As you can already guess, each tab refers to a section of the notebook that you possibly would like to pay attention to. For example, if one tab refers to your grocery list and you need to do your grocery, you can click on this and scan through it instead of having one long list of not only your grocery list but also the other things that you plan on doing.

If in case you have created new tabs but cannot find it in the multiple notebooks that you already have, simply go to Quick Notes because this is where the new notes are placed.

Share Your Notebook

In case you would like other people to have an input about the notebook that you have made, then you can simply share it with other people. After some time, you can also see their own creative input on the notes that you have placed.

Understanding Different Versions of OneNote

OneNote has a variety of versions depending on the operating system. The complete OneNote version runs on Windows.

Windows Version

If you use Windows on a touch screen enabledlaptop or computer, you will be able to use OneNote in the best possible way. The application allows you to take notes with a stylus, and if you wish, you can convert them to text so that the next time youwant to refer to them, they are there.

You can use inking toolstohighlight text for emphasis. You mayadd circles or squares depending on how you think the details should be highlighted. You may also embed files that you alreadyhave in Microsoft Office to OneNote so you access this data fast whenever you need to. It is possible to embedExcel sheets, thoughof smaller sizes.

Without using an application such as OneNote, you might find it challenging to keep data in separate files. Your data would get all mixed up. With OneNote, you have the power to keepyour itemsinseparate files and update them on a regular basis. Though a Windows phone is designed to do all these things,installing the OneNote application enhances its ability to organize data.

iOS Version
The iOS version of OneNote comes with handwriting features that convert written notes to text. A user has the option to convert the text or leave as it is. This may then be linked to personal or business accounts. It is ideal for capturing good moments or sharing funny images with other people without mixing them up with other work related items. Previously, it was difficult to use OneNote on iOS devices due to small screens. However, this has changed in a significant way as larger iOS devices became available in the market.

Android Version
Android offers the latest version of OneNote. It is a direct competition to GoogleKeep, which offers seemingly similar functions. Unlike on iOS, OneNotecan create different widgets thatallow you to access the notes you need immediately by simply scribbling or placing a code. You can also take pictures with your phone and addthemtothe application. In case, you opt to be reminded of your notes, and you own an Android watch, you may choose to access such notes on your watch. This OneNote feature on Android platforms makes everything highly accessible.

Mac Version

Though the Mac version is somewhat similar to OneNote'sWindows version, a fewnoticeable differences are observed.The Mac version allows for sharing of notes with other people but does not allow users to add multiple accounts. This means that one has to choose whether they only want to create a personal notebook or a work notebook.

Now that you know the various OneNote versions available, you can decide which version is most helpful to you and make an informed choice. You will also find it easier to tackle problems that come your way, depending on which platform you use. Not to mention, the work is saved seamlessly and could be accessed through any device that you are already signed in.

Summary

A quick recap of the chapter.

- OneNote, the notes organizing feature by Microsoft, offers a range of services from taking notes, capturing screens, adding audio files and memos, or just doodling.
- It is available across platforms, be it Android, iOS, Mac or Windows.
- It syncs seamlessly across devices, and your notes are available on whatever device you want them to be.

Chapter 2: Basic and Advanced Features of OneNote

This section serves two purposes: outlining what the basic, and the advanced features of OneNote are. This should help you start using OneNote effectively. To begin with, you need to install OneNote in your device – whether laptop, tablet, phone or desktop computer, to be able to use the features that come with it. As a user of this application, it is important that you learn some details about the application. Here is some important information about OneNote:

Essential Details
Manufacturer: Microsoft
Category: Office Applications
Sub - Category: Management of Documents, Office Applications
Initial Release of Software: November 19, 2003
Latest Release: September 22, 2015
Compatible Operating Systems: Microsoft Windows, Android, iOS, Windows Phone, OS - X
Licensing: Media-less

If you are looking to make use of this application for note taking, it is critical that you check your operating system for compatibility. You also need to be aware of system requirements that the application is designed to run on. Having this information enables you to ensure that your device will be able to run the application without any problems. Here are the system requirements that your device needs to meet to run theOneNote app:

System Requirements

To run OneNote, your operating system should be Microsoft Windows 7 or later, Microsoft Windows Server 2008 R2, Microsoft Windows Server 2012.
Other additional system requirements include a 1280 x 800 monitor resolution, compatible graphics card (DirectX 10.0). A touch-enabled screen that makes the use of this application much easier.

Once you verify that your device meets these system requirements, you are ready to download and install OneNote. If your device does not meet theserequirements, you may have to upgrade or get a different device that meets these specifications.

Downloading and InstallingOneNote

To get the application running on your device, here is what you need to do:

- Go to www.onenote.com and click free download if you would like to get it for free
- Install the software
- Launch the software
- Click the notebook tab above the main pane
- Select add notebook
- Click the 'save' button to save it on your gadget or OneDrive folder

Note: If you are using Windows 10 OS on your electronic device, OneNote is already pre-installed so you need not to download and install again. The full version of the application is available when you purchase Microsoft Office 2016; it is part of the bundle.

Formatting Files on OneNote

Whenever a notebook created with OneNote is stored in the computer or OneDrive, the file gets the extension .one. The file size of OneNote is upgraded twice. Files created using OneNote 2003 cannot be edited in updated versions such as 2007, 2010 and 2016. Notebooks created using 2007 and 2010 OneNote versions can be opened as long as their properties are changed.

Getting Started
Once you are ready to start using OneNote, go ahead and create an account with Microsoft. If you use Outlook to manage your e-mails, oryou have purchased the full version of Microsoft Office 2016, you do not need to create a new account, just log in.

Once you log into your new account, you will have access to different features including notebooks, tabs, and pages. Here are some basic features and how to get started with your OneNote application:

Creating a notebook
By following the steps below, you will learn that creating your own Personal Notebook is not the toughest thing you have ever done. In fact, it is simple to get started with OneNote. All you need to do is:

1. Select file then New.
2. Select computer,
3. Enter a name for the notebook.
4. Select 'create in different folder', locate your P:\ drive and select 'SELECT'. (N.B.: Remember always to save your Notebooks to your P; \ drive so that you will not lose them if something happens to the computer).
5. Select Create Notebook.

Follow the steps below to learn how to create a Shared Notebook;

1. Select **file** then **New.**
2. Select **Computer.**
3. Enter a name for the Notebook.
4. Select **Create in a different folder** thenfind the location on a shared drive where you want to save the file and select **Select.**
5. Select **Create Notebook.**

Typing Notes
When you want to take notes,

- Click anywhere on the page.
- Start typing!
- It is as simple as that. Remember a note container will be availableso follow it all the time as you type.Type anywhere on the page to create a new note

Creating Bullet Lists
To create a bullet list:

- Press the asterisk button first, thenstart typing Press the space bar to create a new line.

Creating Numbered Lists
If you want to create a list of numbers instead of bullets,

- Write 1,thenstart typing Press the space bar every time you want to add new numbers to your list.

Handwriting Notes
There are times when you will want to draw or scribble rather than type. To do this, follow these steps

- On the ribbon, click on the 'Draw' button

- More tools will be displayed so you can choose the color and thickness you want to use to write
- If you want to convert your handwritten notes to text, highlight them first,select draw then ink thetext. Check if your handwritten notes have been converted perfectly. Ensure that your handwritten notes are legible, otherwise they will not be saved correctly.

Saving a Notebook

Once you have created your Notebook, there is no need to save it as OneNote saves all your notes automatically as you enter them on the page. This is a good thing because it saves you the trouble of having to remember to save your work as you hurry to beat deadlines or rush to some other meeting.

Organizing your Notebook

Add sections

1. Right- Click on any Section tabs and select **New Section**.
2. Enter a name for the new Section and press Enter on the keyboard.

Add pages

1. Click on Add Page at the top of the Pages list.
2. Enter a page title on the line at the top of the Page. You will see this the "the Weekly Meeting Minutes" appear in the Pages list

We now need to advance you to learn how to move the Sections and Pages you have created.

Move Sections

1. To move a Section within the same 'Notebook':
   a. Click and drag the Section across the top to the new location.

2. To move a Section to a different Notebook;
   a. Click the drop-down arrow next the Notebook name.
   b. Click on the push pin icon to pin the list of the Notebooks to the left side of the screen.
   c. Click and drag the Section you want to move to a different Notebook.

Move Pages
1. To move a Page within the same Section:
   a. Click and drag the Page to a different position in the Pages list.
2. To move a Page to a different Section:
   a. Click and drag the Page to the Section Tab. The Page will be added automatically to the bottom of the Pages list for that Section.
3. To move a Page to a different Notebook:
   a. Click on the drop-down arrow next to the Notebook name.
   b. Click on the push pin icon to pin the list of notebooks to the left side of the screen.
   c. Click and drag the Page to a Section in a different Notebook.

Search for a notebook
OneNote offers search capabilities that let you quickly find specific content within a selected search scope, such as a notebook. As you type more characters in the search box, the results narrow. Links within the results take you to the pages on which the search items appear.

Share a notebook
The ability to create a shared notebook is a big advantage of OneNote over traditional note-taking systems. Many people

can easily access the same OneNote notebook at the same time. Any changes or additions they make are saved automatically. OneNote notebooks can be shared on the Web using Windows Live or via a network. When you share a notebook, OneNote prompts you to send an email message to the people who now have access to it.

Quick Notes

Now after tackling the Pages and learning how to create, save and organize your Notebook, we need to learn how to make Quick Notes. Quick notes are what you use when you are in a hurry, or you don't know yet where to place your notes. You put the Pages with your notes in the Quick Notes area. You can always move your Pages from the quick notes area to a Notebook once you have identified where it belongs.

Taking notes- Adding a text

To add a text in your page, you click on the screen and begin to typing. Each time you click on a different area to start typing a new note container is created. These notes containers can then be moved around the screen by clicking on the text and using the handle at the top to drag the container to a new location.

Adding pictures or Screen Clippings

You will find that at times you will need to include pictures or screen clippings in your notes to enable you to put your point across. Screen clipping are what we commonly refer to as 'screenshots'. How to go about it? See below.

1. Select the 'Insert tab'.
2. To insert a Picture;
   a. Select a picture you want
   b. Locate your picture and insert Open.

3. To insert a screen clipping, commonly known as a (screen shot);
   a. Select screen clipping
   b. Click and drag the crosshair pointer around the section of the screen you would like to capture.
   c. The screen clipping will automatically be placed onto the current Page.

Adding Links

When working on your quick notes, you will find that you might need to add links to a website to your notes for an easier referral. It is not as hard as it is something that you learn quickly, and it is very vital.

1. Add a link to a website;
   a. Copy and paste, or type the website link just like you would for any other text but you should always make sure to include HTTP:// when you enter the text otherwise it will not be easy to click on the link.
2. Add a link to another Page or Section of your Notebook;
   a. Right-click over the page or Section and select Copy Link to Page.
   b. Go to the page where you want to place the link.
   c. Right click and select the first paste icon on the side of the screen.

Adding tables is also essential for you to learn in order to enjoy using your OneNote. You start by;

1. Selecting the Insert tab.
2. Select a table.
3. Then select the size of the table you would like to add.
4. Then there will appear a blank table with a number of rows and columns on the page.

If you are keen enough, you will notice that OneNote is fun to have but there are a lot of things you still need to learn in order to enjoy using OneNote efficiently.

Adding tags

These can be used to easily find important items in your notes.

1. Select the text that you would like to be tagged.
2. Select the Home tag.
3. In the Tag section, select a tag from the list or create a custom tag.

How to tag a note

When you work with a large notebook or with several notebooks, tags provide an option for locating information. Any piece of content can be tagged. For example, you might want to tag notes that are to-do items or contacts, or maybe websites that you wish to visit.

OneNote tags can be searched and sorted.

How to search for tags;

1. Select the Home tab.
2. In the Tag section, select Find Tags.
3. In the Tag Summary section opens, and you can see the tags by Tags Name, Section, Title, Date, or Note Text.

OneNote's Advanced Features

If you have reached this point, you are done with the basic features on the OneNote. You now need to move a step forward to the more advanced features of the OneNote. This is where we learn about calculators and how to use them, drawing tools, outlook, password protect sections, recording audio/video, searching notes, sending emails and to the word, and templates.

Calculator

This will ensure that you can quickly and easily calculate numbers and basic math functions in OneNote.

1. You first enter the calculation (i.e. 3+3=),
2. After the equal sign(=), press on the space bar,
3. The answer you get on the calculation will then appear.

Drawing Tools

Drawing tools are essential to make simple diagrams in your notes. At times, illustrations work best in explaining some points. To access the drawing tools, select the Draw tab.

1. First of all, you choose what you want to do:
    I. **Type:** Use this to enter text and select the note containers.
    II. **Lasso Select:** Use this to select large areas of text or shapes.
    III. **Panning Hand**: Use this to freely and quickly move around the page without using the scroll bars.
    IV. Select the line thickness and color to use for drawing.
    V. Select a pre-built(existing) shape and insert

Outlook-Creating tasks

You can mark items in your notes as Outlook tasks so that you receive reminders in Outlook. This will make sure that every task you have pending and is to be reviewed at a later time is not forgotten as you have it on a reminder.

1. Select the text in your notes that you would like to make an Outlook task.
2. Select the Home tab.
3. In the Tags section, on the farthest left side of your screen, select Outlook Tasks and then select a task completion date.

How to create Linked Notes

You can now link your OneNote notes to meeting appointments in Outlook. You must note that this will however not work with Outlook Web Application (OWA). You must always use the desktop version of Outlook for easier access.

1. In Outlook, you should select the meeting appointment you want to link to OneNote notes,
2. Select Meeting Notes from the Appointment tab.
3. Then select the Notebook or section you want to link to the meeting appointment the select OK.

How to Password protect your sections

It is very vital that you password protect sections in your OneNote Notebooks. This is to make it impossible for someone to mess with your files or notes should they get your access to your gadget. You first of all need to learn how to so it;

1. Right-click on the Section tab you want to password protect.
2. Select Password Protect This Section.
3. Select Set Password.
4. Then enter the password twice to confirm and select OK. You are now good to go.

Learning how to record Audio/ Video

Did you know that you can also record audio and video from

your OneNote into your notes? Well, this is quite possible as long as you a microphone and/or a webcam. Follow the steps on how to go about recording the video/audio.

1. Select the insert tab.
2. Go to select Record Audio (audio only) or Record Video (audio and video).
3. The audio/video will begin to record automatically.
4. When you are done recording, press STOP.
5. You will notice that a link to the audio/video will be placed in your notes. Press the Play button to hear or view the recording.

Searching for Notes

You simply need to 'Enter' the test you want to find in the Search box. A list of all locations will then appear in the drop-down box below the Search Box. Matching text on the current page will then be highlighted in yellow and from there; you can choose what it is you were looking for.

Sending pages from your notes to email

Did you know that you can send a page of your notes to an email so that you can easily share those notes with others? How to go about it:

1. Go to the page you want in an email.
2. Select the Home tab.
3. Select the Email page.
4. A new email will open with contents of the OneNote page. You can also add additional text to the email if the need arises.
5. Enter the email you want to send to in the 'To' field.
6. Then select send.

Converting OneNote 2010 to OneNote 2007

If you have been using OneNote for an extended period of

time, and you have notes you would like to share across the 2010 and 2007 version, here's how to convert your files Convert your OneNote 2010 file to 2007:

- Open the File Menu
- Select 'Properties'
- Click 'Convert to 2007'
- Be patient, it may take a few seconds or minutes to convert depending on the size of the file.
- To reverse the file to OneNote 2010, follow the same process but click 'Convert to 2010' instead of 'Convert to 2007'.

Synchronizing Notes from Android Devices to a Computer

It is important to always remember that for easy syncing, you need to ensure that everything is set up correctly. Follow the following steps to synchronize your Android to properly synchronize your Android device with your computer::

- Make sure you have OneNote 2010, 2013 or 2016. Earlier versions will not sync properly with Android devices
- Open the notebook on your computer and click on 'File' then 'Share'
- Choose a location for your notebook
- Click 'Add a Place'
- Sign into OneDrive

To check your Android phone:

- Log onto your Microsoft account via the web browser on your phone
- Find the notebook you want to sync
- Open the OneNote

Sending pages from your Notes to Word

Equally, it is possible to send pages of your Notes to a Word document;

1. Go to the page you want to send to Word.
2. Select 'File'.
3. Select 'Send'.
4. Select 'Send to Word'.
5. A word document will then open with contents of the OneNote page.

Templates

OneNote includes several templates to help avoid retyping common information as well as enhancing the look of the pages. Templates make your work look more organized and easier for you to access.

1. Select the Insert tab.
2. Select Page Templates.
3. You can now choose a template from the list of available templates.
4. When you click on template title, a new page is created with the selected template.

OneNote includes built-in templates for organizing and adding visual interest to the pages of a notebook. The templates in OneNote are categorized as:

- Academic
- Blank
- Nosiness
- Decorative
- And planners.

You should know that you can apply a template only into a new page. You cannot apply a template to an existing page.

How to take a Screenshot

OneNote allows users to take screenshots when needed. There are times when you need to capture screens of notes you have taken. In this case, you need to know how to take screenshots using the OneNote. Here are easy steps to get you started:

- Go to 'Insert' on your MS Office file
- Open OneNote and click on the 'Clip' tool on the toolbar
- Insert screen shot on your notes
- Click the ESC button to abort the situation

Things You Should Be Doing All the Time with Your OneNote

While you may be having a hard time digesting all the things you can do with your OneNote, there are some features that you just cannot miss out on.

They include:

Creating a To-Do List

You can organize the things you want to do throughout the day. To achieve this,go to the home button and select 'To-Do'. Just press the Enter button plus CTRL+1 to add new items to the list.

Doodling and Sketching

The Doodle and Sketch feature isn't always available in other note taking applications but you are sure to find it on OneNote. This feature allows you to sketch not only your thoughts, but it also enables you to sketch ideas. To access this feature, go to the draw tab button and sketch stuff away. The full range of colors in varying thickness allows you to explore your creativity.

Duplicating Writing on Paper

With OneNote, you can get a feel of writing on paper.

- Go to the 'View Tab' of the application
- Choose the type of finish you want on the Grid Lines and Page Color buttons
- Choose the kind of paper you want to use.

You may opt for grid lines that are similar to your math notebook with white paper so you remember how you used to write your math equations.

Adding Multimedia to Notes

In case you are not able to take down notes using OneNote at lighting fast speed, you may choose to use multimedia tools to make this possible. These include the use of audio or video recordings that can easily be inserted in new notes. Here's how to add multimedia files to your notes:

- Select the page where you want to place a media file
- Go to the 'Insert' button and pick the audio or video record depending on what you want to add

Control your audio or video recording using the different buttons available on the application.

Protecting Your Notes

At times you do not want other people to see the notes you have created, so OneNote comes with the option to protect notes. OneNote, allows you to set passwords fast and easy. If you want to protect your notes using passwords, identify the fileyou want protected. Go to the Review tab and choose'Password Protect'. This feature is available in the latest versions of OneNote.

OneNote also has a locking function that automatically locks your computer when youleave it untouched for an extended period of time. You will need to input your password to unlock it. The app saves your notes automatically, another feature that helps in protecting your notes.

A' Save As' button is also available, but you only use this when you want tore name a note so you can find it easily. Other than that, it is not something you need to worry about.

Keyboard Shortcuts

On many occasions, you may need to do things fast on your computer or laptop and keyboard shortcuts are quite useful in this. If you are not working with a touch screen interface, they come in handy.

There are also moments when you want to use a blank page. You can only achieve this by clearing the contents on an open page using a set of commands, tabs and buttons available on the application. Here are some keyboard shortcuts that you can use to do so as you focus on taking or capturing notes:

- Toggle The Ribbon: CTRL+F1
- Toggle Full Screen: F11
- Zoom In: ALT+CTRL+(+)
- Zoom Out: ALT+CTRL+(-)

Of course, there are some commands that will require you to use buttons and tabs. Such include zooming the page to 100% or to fit the screen. To do these things, you will need to click on the 'View' button thenpick an appropriate command.

Summary

There are a host of things you could do using OneNote. The software gives the user an experience of working with a notebook.

- A notebook consists of pages and sections. One can start adding content as it is, or organize it in sections, as one wishes.
- It allows a user to use a range of features like typing, doodling, writing, capturing screens, recording and adding audio and video files and embedding files.
- You can save the notebook on the computer as well as in the cloud, and share pages, sections or even whole notebooks.
- The work can be password protected for added security.
- It gives a user a familiar user interface and the functions are fairly intuitive.

Chapter 3: OneNote's Compatibility

After learning all the basics and features of OneNote, I am sure that you now need the program on your mobile device. This is very easy to do, especially once you have confirmed that your device can handle this program.

Platform Support

OneNote is supported by various platforms. One such platform is Windows Live Mesh that allows people to send their notes to cloud based storage. This means that even if you make notes on another device, whenever the application is downloaded on another device, you will be able to view your written notes on any other computer or any other appliance immediately. Most tablets, laptops, and mobile phones that are Windows supported have the full version of OneNote. Devices that had been released after OneNote 2007 was released into the market came with a pre-downloaded version of OneNote 2007. Devices running on Windows that are currently entering the market come with OneNote 2016.Over the past years, OneNote has been integrated into various operating platforms. Today, OneNote is supported by:

Windows

If you want the full OneNote, you can get it on Windows by choosing the most full-featured version of Microsoft where all once-premium features are now. You should also know that OneNote's closest physical companion is Microsoft's own Surface Pro 3. You can click the top button on the tablet's bundled digital stylus to wake the device, automatically fire up a new note and start inking away. Users with touch screen devices can write notes with a stylus or finger. An entire tab OneNote's Ribbon menu is devoted towards inking tools, including highlight, circle or digitize options.Ifyou are running OneNote on a Windows device, here's how to get things done:

Syncing an Existing Notebook

It is advisable to save a notebook on OneDrive first before syncing it. After that, sign into your Microsoft account on your device. Go to the App List and select OneNote. Here, you will can see notebooks that you have created before. As long as you sync all items appropriately, you will have no trouble opening and editing the notebooks later.

Creating a New Note

If you are looking to create a new note, follow these steps:on your device,

- Open the OneNote app on your device
- Go to the 'New' button You will see an option to add a title. If you choose not to add a title, the first few words of the notes will serve as the title.
- After adding the title, continue typing your notes.

If you have already set up a Microsoft account, the notes you make are automatically saved through OneDrive especially if you work online. If not, a new notebook will be created for you.

To open an existing note, go to the OneNote icon again and select the note that you want to open for editing. Sometimes you might not readily see the available notes. In such cases

- Press the search button

- Tap the page you are searching to open it Tap on recent so you see the latest notes you have created.

You can also open the notes manually by clicking on the notebook where notes have been saved and scanning through the pages until you see the note you are looking for.

Formatting Notes

As you take notes, you might want to emphasize some words or sentences in your notes. OneNote allows you to format such words according to your requirements easily. The application comes with features that are very similar to those offered by Microsoft Office. You can format notes by following these easy steps:

- Tap on the word you wish to emphasize
- Drag the circles from that word
- Tap the 'More' button to choose proper formatting
- Once done, turn off the formatting by selecting the 'More' button again.

Note: Unfortunately for iPad and iPhone users, changing font colors is not possible, but modification of page color is possible.

Sending Notes via E-mail

If you wish to send yourself or someone else a note through e-mail, you can do so by following the following steps:

- Open the OneNote app
- Choose the note you wish to send through e-mail
- Tap the 'More' button, then go to 'Share'
- Select an e-mail account you wish to use send the note.

- Add the e-mail recipients then press 'Send'

Pin Note to Start Screen
If you want to ensure that you can access OneNote immediately you press the start button, you can just pin it. This way, it will be automatically accessible.

Creating Different Kinds of Lists
OneNote allows you to create various lists. You can choose any new note and press the 'to-do' button to create a to-do list.You may also opt to use bullet lists or numbered lists. After placing in the first item, press enter to proceed to the next available item.

Inserting Pictures with OneNote
It is possible to add the photos on OneNote. To do this, tap on the image icon and either choose to take a new picture or save a picture from another source. It may be a bit tricky taking photos with your standard phone camera, but if you opt to take a photo of a whiteboard or documents, ensure you do sousing the Office Lens. This will be discussed in detail later on in this guide.

Adding Audios
In case you want like to add an audio note as opposed to writing notes, you can get this done with ease. First, tap on the audio button and record your audio file. Press the 'Stop' button once you are done.

Using OneNote on your Windows phone is very similar to using it on a desktop computer. However, there are some limitations because it does not have all the features available in OneNote 2016 and OneNote Online.Still, OneNote on Windows phones is very useful in making notes about different things.

Mac

Microsoft recently released an 'OneNote for Mac', bringing it to the OS X desktop for the very first time. The interface, however, is extremely similar to the Windows versions, but there are fewer tabs in the ribbon across the top which, unfortunately, translates to fewer features as compared to the Windows.

OneNote for Mac carries much of the look and feel over from the Windows version.

You should know that the deeper integration with Office and the ability to sign in with multiple accounts, for instance, is only found on the Windows variant, IA web app for chromes.

Do note that when it comes to using OneNote for Mac, users are expected to place a title for each notebook they create so that organizing notebooks becomes easier.

How to Insert Links on OneNote for Mac

If you type text that OneNote recognizes as web links, the app formats the text automatically. This means that website links, appear as they should. This feature of OneNote makes the link clickable even when you have it as part of your notes.

In case the app does not recognize a link immediately, you can opt to copy it in manually. To do this, here is what you need to do:

- Select the text or picture you want to appear as a link in your notes
- Go to 'Insert' and click on the 'Link' button.
- A link dialogue box will appear
- Paste link information in the dialogue box

- Click 'OK'

This will make the link clickable.

Attaching Files to Notes

In the event that you are not familiar with attaching files to notes created with OneNote, you need to follow these steps:

- Choose the page you want to add the file; it may be anywhere.
- Go to the 'Insert' button and click on 'File Attachment'
- Determine the Files you want 'Insert' and select them.
- Click the 'Insert' button

After completing this process, you will see inserted files on the page.

Inserting Images

While videos are not supported by OneNote's Mac version, you canplace imagesin your notes to make them even more interesting. Here are the steps to follow when inserting images to your notes:

- Choose the images you want to place in your notes. This can bean image taken with your phone,downloaded from the internet or images that you have scanned.
- Go to the 'Insert' button and click on the image
- The Picture Dialog Box will open,
- Add the images you wish to place in your notes.

Inserting Tables

It is possible to create or add tapes to notes, to make your notes more organized than usual. To insert a table, you need to create a grid first then customize it according to your requirements. To do this:

- Click on the 'Insert tab 'then go to the 'Table' button
- Choose the number of grids you want based on your needs using your mouse or pointer
- The table will appear on your current page

If you want to add a theme to your notes, you need to design the table in a way that suits the current theme. To do this:

- Select the cells you want to change on the table. You can have more than one color for the table.
- Click on the commands that you wish to apply to the area that you have selected.

Adding Sections to Your iOS OneNote Version
 With an iOS OneNote Version, you can make your entire notebook appear like a binder. This means that you can create unlimited sections, with different color codes in your notebook with ease. If your physical notebook can only carry a maximum of 5 sections, your OneNote will allow you to make as many sections as you like. Here's how to do this:

- Go to the menu bar and click on 'File'
- Choose 'New Section'
- One section will appear on your notebook.
- Give each section a title so you can find it easily

Saving Notes on iOS OneNote Version
To save notes on OneNote, you don't have to click the save button from time to time because as long as it is synced to your OneDrive, it will automatically save your work on its

own. You need not to worry about losing the notes you take because everything will be there when you check on it again. You only need to press the 'Save As' button when you want to rename them differently.

Using Voiceoveron Mac OS X
You can connect your OneNote to voice over so you won't have problems recording audio files. Connecting to voiceoveris ideal when you are not in the mood to type and you need to release your thoughts.

To turn on or turn off voiceover, use the keyboard shortcut,(+) + F5. If you want to do more with the voiceover, press the plus sign + Options + F5. Knowing these keyboard shortcuts allow you to control this better.

iOS
OneNote is the perfect app for writing notes on the run or scribbling quick sketches with your finger or a stylus; this can be enjoyed on the massive iPhone 6 Plus. Like the Windows version, the iOS app connects to both consumer and enterprise accounts making it perfect for capturing those important meeting notes and saving hilarious Buzz feed listicles.
With this app, you can share directly into OneNote from other Apps.

Signing In with Microsoft OneNote
You can only start using Microsoft OneNote on your choice device if you already have an existing Microsoft account. You will be prompted to sign at the moment that you start using it. If you don't get a prompt box:

- Open your OneNote application

- Tap on the button and go toSign In
- Type your e-mail address. You may choose to use your phone number if it's more convenient for you
- Click on the'Next' button
- Key in your Microsoft account and password, then Sign In.

You can use your personal email address to log in to your Microsoft account,as long as you link it to your Microsoft account.

Some Limitations of OneNote for iOS
There are features available on other platforms that are not found in OneNote for iOS. This means that your OneNote usage of iOS becomes limited. Here are some areas where OneNote for iOS is limited:

- The use of audio and video clips
- Math equations
- Creating ink drawings
- Handwritten notes
- Selection of full page

If you have any concerns about OneNote working well on your iPad or iPhone, you need not worry because notes that are created on OneNote will automatically sync with your device. You can sync as many notebooks as you wish from various locations.

Remember notebooks that can be synchronized and supported on your iPad or iPhone are those created using OneNote 2010 and later versions. It is not possible to sync notebooks created in OneNote 2007.

Working Offline

There are times you will opt to work offline.OneNote for iOS allows you to do this with ease.All you need to do is to ensurethat you sync your notebook with OneDrive beforehand so that for every change you make is synced. If you are working online and you lose the internet connection midway as you use your OneNote, your notes will remain intact in the OneDrive.

Turning On Accessibility Options

In case you want to make OneNote easier to access through your iOS powered device, you only need to:

- Change Contrast to High and Increase Page Visibility by:

  1. Going to Settings
  2. Choosing the General Option
  3. Selecting 'Accessibility' and turning on the Voiceover

- Zoom or Magnify Your Screen by

  1. Going to Settings
  2. Choosing General
  3. Selecting 'Accessibility' and clicking on 'Zoom'

Deleting a Page

Deleting unwanted or erroneous pages or notes is always recommended to release space in your device. By deleting such notes you ensure that your device works faster and better. Deleting a note is easy when you follow the following steps:

- Swipe left or right on the page tab

- Then click the'Delete' button

If you delete a page or note unintentionally, just click on the 'undo' button and the page will beavailable again.

If you remove a page and then decide to restore it again after a few days, you can retrieve it from your Recycle Bin. However, you need to bear in mind that your recycle bin is always cleared automatically after 60 days.

IOS users need to note that in order to delete an entire notebook, they'll need a device that runs OneNote on a different operating system. This is because current OneNote for iOS versions do not have this feature.

How to Open Shared Notebooks

If another person shares a notebook with you and you need to open it immediately, you can do this easily by:

- Clicking the 'Open' button to see details about the notebook as well as the name of the person who has shared it with you.
- Tap on the notebook to start reading its contents

In case you open your OneNote application and do not see the notebook, it's probably because you are not logged in to your Microsoft account. The account that you use must be the same account that the person has used to share the notebook.

Content Sharing from Other Applications

Sometimes you will want to find content that is available on other applications and websites. To do this from the OneNote app:

- Clip content from various web pages
- Send formatted text and file attachments
- Save photos on your notebook pages.

Content sharing can be easy as long as your system is running well. To use this unique feature, you need to have the following:

- iOS 8 or a later version
- Sign into OneNote and make sure that one notebook is open
- Enable OneNote to be shared

Once you have checked and confirmed that everything is okay, you can start sharing content by following this simple process:

- Sign into OneNote and open one of the notebooks that you already created
- Tap on the 'Share' menu on your device from which you wish to share content
- Go to the 'More' button
- Display the 'Activities List'
- Go to the 'OneNote' button and tap the slider so that sharing is enabled.

Sharing an Item through OneNote

- Using the app you wish to clip content from, tap on the 'Share' button.
- Go to'OneNote'

- Choose where you would like to place your content. Basically, content can be placed anywhere on the notebook page
- Click on the 'Send' button
- You may also choose to add a note to the content that you are going to share just in case you need a reminder on why you want to place it there

OneNote can also be accessed offline, but you need to make sure you have synced your notebooks to OneDrive first so you can retrieve the files whenever you need them.

If you are using iOS 8, you may organize the applications icons so you can quickly tap on those that you use for sharing. If you opt to do it manually, long press the icon and move it to another location.

Android

It is interesting that as much as Android is an arch-rival of Microsoft, it still supports OneNote. OneNote can easily be downloaded on Google play as it does not come automatically with the phone.

Installing OneNote on Android

If you are interested in installing OneNote on Android within the shortest possible time, you should have an operating system running Android 4.0 or a later version. You should also have a Smartphone that already has camera and voice recorder capabilities. As always, to use OneNote, you need to have a Microsoft account. You also need to have an account with Office 365.

What to Expect from OneNote on Android

Here are some key features that you will enjoy on OneNote

once you have it running on your Android phone:

- Create notebooks using Android devices
- Share web content, images, voice recordings and more with other OneNote users
- Check recent notes by adding the OneNote widget on your home screen
- Type in notes the way you want. You may choose to bold, italicize and underline some words that you use in your notes.
- Sync work notes with share point online sites

Removing Badge Notification
If you do not want to receive any notifications regarding software updates or any other information about the notes that you create, you will need to do away with badge information in your tray. To get this done:

- Open OneNote
- Click on the 'Overflow' menu
- Choose 'Settings'
- Go to 'Add OneNote to Notification Tray.'
- Uncheck the option

Opening a Notebook with SharePoint
If youopt to open your notebook or someone else's notebook through SharePoint, you need to have the complete SharePoint URL. Without this, you will not be able to open the notebook on your Android phone. SharePoint is generally easier to access through a computer or any other Android device.

Creating New Notes without Opening Application

When you don't want to go through the process of opening an application just to create notes, you can make a short and quick note. With Android devices, this is possible as long as you have the OneNote widget readily available on your home screen.

Troubleshooting

Recently, there was an update on OneNote for Android. Some users have started complaining that the notes go missing or some of the stuff they write get marked even when they know they have not marked it.

One way to stop this from happening is installing the latest updates and syncing all notes. This way, the notes will not be placed under the misplaced section in OneNote where all notes are 'read only.' In case you need to edit the file that has been moved to the lost section, your only option is to copy the notes manually. This gets a bit complicated, especially when the notes are long.

Editing a Notebook or Page

In case you experience trouble with editing a notebook or a page through your Android phone, do not panic. Instead, think of possible reasons why your notebook or page does not work. These may include

- You are trying to edit an e-mail attachment. Though there is a lot that OneNote can do, it cannot edit pages or notebooks sent through e-mail yet.
- The notebook or page you are trying to open is a 'read–only' file
- Your phone does not support the notebook or the page you are trying to edit.

- The notebook file may be corrupted and can no longer be opened.
- The password set on the notebook is hindering you from opening and editing it

Check your notebook or pages for any of these issues and resolve them in order to continue editing.

Recovering notes that are not synced

In the event that you work offline to and take notes and were not able to sync them properly, OneNote allows you to recover them. Below are steps to help you recover any notes that are not synced:

- Start your OneNote from Recent Notes
- Wait until OneNote syncs all the notes you have created Note that some notes will be placed in the misplaced section. Such notes end up being in read-only mode.
- Wait till all notes are thoroughly synced. You may want to check your notebook and pages to see when the sync button stops flashing on the screen
- Go to the misplaced section to find copies of the notes you forgot to sync
- You may copy them manually and place each in a new note, then sync again so they are editable.

As you may have come to learn, OneNote is heaven sent as it is has come to make lives a little bit easier and more manageable. We all want to be organized and efficient at our jobs and what better way than by having a tool that can help you in creating and storing important information that you might require to use at a later date. Any kind of information you store on OneNote will not be lost, and this makes it more valuable as it reduces your stress levels, therefore, making you more relaxed and fit to do other things.

OneNote keeps the flood of information neat and tidy and accessible as they are stored in the cloud. This app is better as a productivity aide, with its focus on typing and handwriting notes, audio recording, and numerous search tools and with a smart integration with the rest of Office.

OneNote has a clearly defined organizational structure that mimics physical note-taking, revolving around notebooks, tabs, and pages. It has good organizational structure that makes is easy to keep everything in it place, a fact that can be emphasized over and over again.

OneNote makes it easier for one to have multiple notebooks. This makes it possible for one to divide up work tasks. OneNote comes pre-installed for people who use the Windows Phone, therefore, no stress in downloading the app.
The thought of having all your work that can amount to numerous pages of actual papers into one very small gadget is amusing in itself. I mean, you no longer have to walk around with unfinished work in your briefcase or anything....luggage is the one thing that today's generation detest. So by having this information on your phone that you never leave behind makes it possible for you to attend to your work anywhere anytime. This is a sweet relief.

Chronology of One Note Versions Many people may not be aware that OneNote has been around since 2003. It first started as a simple note taking application but over the years, it has improved to become the OneNote version that can perform a wide range of tasks as we know today. Here's how

OneNote has changed over time.

OneNote 2003
In the year 2003, OneNote only allowed users to create notes offline. The app had not been integrated into online note taking just yet. Users were not authorized to create tables and headings and files could only be saved in one format.

OneNote 2007
In 2007, an improved version was launched. While the 2007 OneNote version could still not support online notebooks, users were allowed to create local notebooks that allowed them to take notes with ease. They could place tables and headings though the colors would remain the same. They could add titles yet, but they were allowed to protect their files using passwords.

OneNote 2010
This was the first OneNote version to allow for the creation of online notebooks. Users were allowed to add headings and some notebook sections could be password protected as well. One notable feature about the 2010 OneNote version is its ability to integrate Word, Excel and other documents. Users can integrate their files and save them in OneNote 2010 format. 2007 OneNote files can also open on the 2010 version as the files are automatically upgraded.

OneNote 2013
When this version first came into the market in 2013, there was a lot of confusion because different versions OneNote versions had already been released previously. OneNote 2013 Volume Version is the full version that allows notebooks to be opened through a SharePoint Server. Like in the other earlier versions, creating tables is possible only

with this version.It is also possible to change colors on tables.

Another OneNote version released in 2013 is the click-to-run version. This version can be downloaded directly from the website. While it contains some of the features found in the full version, it does not support third party links which means that users cannot link it to PDF.

Since there is a full version available of which the click-to-go version is a derivative, it is good to know that a free version is available, outside the suite. To create online notebooks, one has to log in. Creating offline notebooks is not possible with the Click-To-Go version as it does not have the features that a full version has.

OneNote 2016
Several versions of OneNote were released in the year 2016. Like the 2013 version, there a full version or the premium version, the click-to-run version and a free version were released in this year.

The full 2016 version allows users to create both offline and online notebooks and notes. This version enhances note taking processed by linking to various software like Microsoft Word and PowerPoint. Users can also take screenshots. It is important to take note that this version, and all other OneNote 2016 versions cannot be installed on computers that run on Windows XP operating system.

The Click-To-Run version is available for downloading for installation from the official website.

While it is very similar to the full version, it cannot be linked to other third party websites and software for note taking.

The free version of OneNote 2016comes with limited features compared to the other two versions. Users can only create one notebook on one drive since the one they get is free. Still, one can expect to get all the necessary functions they are looking for in the search for the right version of OneNote. Just recently, the free version was updated and the restrictions removed. Elimination of restrictions means that users can attach files and create passwords to protect their notes.

As you can see, OneNote has undergone various changes over the years with Microsoft making an effort to understand the needs that users have in note taking and improving the application to meet those needs.

Summary
OneNote is available across platforms. That said, the availability of features on each platform differ slightly. This has to do with the availability of hardware, the native fidelity of Microsoft products to Windows Operating system and user interfaces.

- Windows offers the most comprehensive set of features, especially when available with a touch screen interface.
- iOS and Mac offer a few features less, like deleting documents on iOS, or fewer ribbon options on Mac.
- Android users would have an experience that differs from device to device.
- The latest versions of OneNote offer more flexibility overall, so upgrading it is recommended.
- A click-to-run version is available, which is essentially a free version with a limited set of features.

Chapter 4: Reasons You Need Microsoft OneNote

Microsoft OneNote has unique organizational features that help its users to keep data at hand and easy to retrieve at all times. It has so many benefits to any user as discussed here:

Information Storage and Retrieval Software

Microsoft OneNote is amazing information storage and retrieval software. Storing information is important to any individual, business or organization. Every day, people are creating information ofall manners and it is just right to have a proper storage for this information in case it will be needed in the future.

OneNote does not only make it easier for the user to create the information and store it but also to retrieve it. What you need to do is to save all the information in unique manner and when it is needed, you just type one unique word and you will have all the information you have saved in the past.

The software also keeps records of all the details of stored information just in case this will be needed. You do not need another information storage and retrieval means when this software is available.

Collaboration Software

The use of Microsoft OneNote in an office setting allows different people to access information and data easily in the office. Multiple users of the same network can easily access the same kind of information with ease, without necessarily having to share it out and waste so much time and energy.

If changes are needed in the information that has already been created, anyone within that network can easily do that. OneNote will show all these changes and the author so that anyone that will come across the changes will know who changed the information, when it was changed and other relevant details.

OneNote has a web app and a mobile app that you can use so as to share out and access shared information with ease even when you are on the go.

OneNote's Multimedia Capabilities

Most productivity software focuses on only one type of file but OneNote is different; it works with the most common data formats and it can import and receive different kinds of media. Some of the formats that are compatible with OneNote include Excel, Word and PowerPoint documents.
You can also upload a media directly to OneNote using a webcam or a microphone that is already attached and share it out to different platforms with ease.

Office Integration Made Easier

OneNote is a part of the office Program Suite and so, it uses the same interface with other office programs. This makes it easy for users of office suite programs to access the options of OneNote. OneNote is able to send and receive files and documents from other Office programs and even send and receive emails from Outlook. It is a program that is meant to make things very easy for the Office Suite users. This is just what office workers need so as to enjoy the convenience.

Clipping the Web is Possible

When you come across an important document or image online that you would like to save in your personal notebook or work notebook, you can easily clip it to OneNote and check it later. The app allows you to view clipped pages and images later, both online and offline.

Send E-Mails for Note Integration

When you want to add details to your OneNote, but does not have the time to integrate it into your notebook, you can make additions as long as you e-mail it to me@onenote.com.Once you do this, the details will be placed in your notebook. To make use of this feature, you need to set up your e-mail first.

Take Clear Photos

In case you need to take photos of your documents or whiteboards containing written text, use Office Lens. Unlike taking pictures with a phone camera, using Office Lens gives your documents scan like quality, and every detail in the document is legible.To use Office lens, here is what you need to do:

- Create or open a new note
- Tap on the note to access the keyboard
- Tap on the Camera icon
- Pic the picture mode you want to use from the optionsavailable, namely Whiteboard, Photo and Document.
- Take the picture.
- Tap and save the image in your note.

This tool can be extremely useful, particularly if you always lose business cards handed to you by potential clients. Instead of sifting through piles of paper trying to locate business cards, simply take a photo of the business card and have it readily available on your OneNote app whenever you need it. You may also convert images to PDF if you so wish.

The Use of OneNote for Personal Gain

If you are looking for software that will ease your life, Microsoft OneNote is the right one for you. It can literally take care of your note-taking needs, among other needs. While some users only take advantage of the simple things they can do with this program, others are exploring other great things that they can do with it in order to explore its full effectiveness.

Some personal gains you can get from OneNote are:
- ✓ Reduced stress from creating and organizing notes all by yourself
- ✓ Becoming more organized in every sense of the way. There is so much that you can do with OneNote to stay organized everyday
- ✓ Save your time for other things. Instead of spending so much time organizing notes and data and looking for previously created notes and data, you could be doing something more important. This makes this software a great savior.

Here are some tips that can help you get more out of your OneNote:
i) Start by getting OneNote for free! If you are using Windows 8, iOS, Android or Windows Phone, you can use OneNote for free. The version that you will get will not be as functional as the one that you will get in the Microsoft Office suite but there are official apps that are available for these platforms that you can use to access all the features that OneNote has.

ii) Sync All Your Notes. This will save you so much time and frustration as you can manage all your notebooks from the different devices that you may have in one central location. This is also meant to save your day and makes things very easy for you. Once you sync all your notebooks, you can access them in their recent format from any mobile device or computer.

iii) Get organized. OneNote is not to be used entirely for note taking but also for storing important information in your life and organizing it. Use it to create and organize your To-Do-Lists for instance, shopping lists, organizing a research when planning a trip or even organizing your client's information for business. This is a program that you can use absolutely for anything that you find important in your life, whether long term or short term.
The program does not only allow you to make notes and create data but also to keep it organized for easier retrieval. It is a very useful program.

iv) Ease Your Student Life. OneNote is a program that will really benefit a student. If you are a student and you haven't had time to use one, you are missing out on so many things.
The program has the best organizational structure for taking notes and it can organize your notes per lecture, topic or even class. It also has amazing feature that a student will find really useful. For instance homework lists, lecture notes, quick notes, reviews and so many others.

You are also able to synch information so that you can access your data from anywhere whenever you are on the go.

v) Do Math on your notes. There are a few features that so many people have not discovered yet that makes OneNote more useful, for instance its ability to take care of mathematical problems on your notes. This is a feature that will make things much easier for you when you are taking notes. This feature covers a very wide mathematical area and if you are using the paid version of the program, be assured that you will access more mathematical functions that will allow you to do even more on your notes.

OneNote is, therefore, software that is worth a try if you have not been using it. It deserves more exploration too if you have not been using it fully. This is software that will make things easier and happier for you and boost transparency in an organization since information can flow easily from one person to the other.

Pros and Cons of OneNote
The applications like OneNote are created and features are added taking into account the evolving needs of the user. It is, thus fair to say that such applications, including OneNote, are not exactly perfect. While this application is designed to offer users a wide array of features that they look for, it is important that theyare aware of its limitations so they know what to expect. Here are the pros and cons of OneNote applications:

Pros:

- **The Stack Interface:** Whether you have been using OneNote for a long time or you are just getting started, you can tell that the interface makes the whole application user-friendly. No matter what platform you run the app on, you can be assured that it will be easy to figure out.

- **Color Divider:**If you want everything color coded, OneNote app is able to do this and enhance your ability to keep things organized. The app also enables you to organize individual tabs using color codes so they are easy to find based on their colors.

- **Easy to Run on All Devices:** If you have a Windows powered laptop, or even a Mac powered one, you can run the OneNote app. The app also runs on all phone platforms are available in the market. Though the features may differ a bit depending on the platform designs, most tend to be more compatible with Windows version of OneNote. However, the app can generally run on any platform.

- **Elegant Look:** Everyone wants to use an application that looks good. OneNote comes with a simple but elegant look that appeals to most users.

- **Easy to Integrate with Other Documents:** If you want to place a portion ofcontent fromWord filesto notebooks that you have created, or vice versa, OneNote allows you to do this with relative ease. The latest versions of OneNote are integrated with MS Word and Excel, an aspect that allows users to add Excel files to OneNote and review them from the app.

Cons:

- **Newbies May Find OneNote Hard to Understand in the Beginning:** New users are likely to find OneNote tricky to understand. This is especially true for the Windows version that comes with a wide variety of improved features. It might be a bit complicated in the beginning, but after spending time interacting with the application, one becomes accustomed to it and finds it easier to use.

- **The Application is not the same for all platforms:** OneNote does not use the same design across all operating systems and phone platforms. The features vary from one platform to another. Each operating system has its own design, an aspect that presents a challenge to people who want to use it on different platforms. On the Windows operating system, users are able to do more with OneNote compared to Mac or iOS platforms. For instance, the Mac version is less than stellar because of the limited features available.

- **Mac Users cannot Embed Videos:** While it is possible to add files, text and other details on notes created on OneNote, users cannot add videos to the Mac version of this application. This feature is only available in the Windows version of OneNote.

Add-Ins for One-Note

In addition to the rich feature capabilities within the app itself, OneNote has great Add-Ins that have been developed by individuals to make your note taking even more powerful. There are several available, but one in particular adds several valuable features.

OneTastic is a great example of an Add-In for OneNote. This application allows for macros to be used to automate/schedule tasks. It also allows your notes to display in a calendar view. It provides the capability to also crop/rotate images and many other valuable features that make it a good addition to the OneNote capabilities.

Here is a quick list of others you might want to use:
OneNote Class – Helps you organize class content (designed for teachers/instructors)
Office Lens – use your smartphone to capture physical whiteboards, etc. into your OneNote application.

Look around for additional add-ins that offer extended functionality to enhance your OneNote experience.

Chapter 5: Comparison of OneNote with Other Applications

Comparison of One Note with EverNote

The release of OneNote was direct competition for another application referred to as EverNote, is interesting considering how popular EverNote has been. EverNote has dominated the market for a very long time, but it was about time to release a program that will cover up some of the shortcomings of EverNote. The two programs have been designed to work on the same platforms but they have very distinctive features, which makes OneNote much better than the popular EverNote in one sense and EverNote better than OneNote in the other sense.

OneNote is a great way to get organized, something that EverNote does not offer to its users. With OneNote, you can create simple to complex notes from the beginning, organize them into notebooks that can be searched and browsed and even make them accessible through different platforms through synchronization. You can easily access your notes, plus all their details from OneNote with little or no effort.

OneNote's note creation tools are much more advanced than those of EverNote. If you are the kind of user that needs software that will create great quality notes and help you organize them, you will be much better using OneNote. However, it is incapable of clipping notes from the internet like EverNote and this is its main shortcoming.

OneNote gives its users access to many different kinds of features and this means that it is much more useful than its counterpart. If you are looking for software that will give you more benefits between the two, it is best to go for OneNote but always remember that there are features from EverNote that you may not get from OneNote.

However, if you are looking for software that will also allow you to find, capture and organize content from the internet, OneNote will not be great for this, but EverNote.

Both EverNote and OneNote is note taking tools but their features make them so different in what they offer to their clients. You will choose what to go for depending on what you want to achieve. The good thing is that you can always use both of them for their different features so as to ensure that you are achieving more every day and making things easier for yourself.

Why OneNote is better than EverNote?

OneNote and EverNote are two applications that compete to become market leaders in the note taking space. These two note taking applications tend to be compared to each other often because they tend to appeal to various users and each has features that gives it an edge. Most importantly, there are functions that OneNote can perform that EverNote currently cannot.

Such functions include adding text to files, adding images and doodling and writing ideas that come to mind. A lot of the functionality in OneNote depends on a user's ability to personalize it, which makes itbetter than EverNote. Here are details of what a user can do using OneNote, differently than when he uses EverNote.

Integrating Office
Unlike EverNote, integration with Office is possible with

OneNote. This is perhaps the case because EverNote is not connected to other software like OneNote is to Office. With the former, users cannot include Word documents but this is easy to do with OneNote.

Adding Videos to Notes

When using the OneNote for Windows, one can take notes in a different waycompared to how they take down notes using traditional methods, Instead of drawing comic strips to keep things interesting, you can easily add videos to your notes and make things work well for you. This is not the case with the EverNote app.

Keep To Do Lists Organized

You can expect that aside from your OneNote notebook, there is a lot more to do with the app like ensuring lists are organized. This is easily achieved by adding tabs to pages of a notebook. Users can also compare their lists using sticky notes if they so wish. On OneNote, sticky notes may be placed just like they are added on a typical notebook.

GetAdditional Storage for Free

For those who take notes on different things and need plenty of space, OneNote comes in handy. The app offers users free storage space of up to 15 GB with ease. This amount of space is not bad at all when you think of how much text and images you need to generate to fill it up.

From the things are mentioned above, it is evident that OneNote offers a lot of things that EverNote app cannot.

Comparison of OneNote with Google Keep

While people never thought that Google Keep will be revived by Google again, the app was coming back to the market to compete with EverNote as well as OneNote. The Google Keep app is available to users for free when used online as well as for download on Android powered devices.

On the other hand, OneNote is part of the Microsoft Office 365 subscription. It can come as part of the package when purchased alongside other applications that are useful in devices. Like Google Keep, OneNoteis can be used for free online. Afree version of the app is also available for users who do not wish to spend money on it. The OneNote Office version is considered better compared to other versions because it has the ability to take screenshots that can be printed out directly.

So far, Google Keep does not have applications that can be used on Android and iOS devices. What this means is that users can only access and use it online with either a laptop or desktop computer. Eventually, Google might release something similar to what OneNote is already offering to the general public, but for now, it is evident that OneNote is the perfect choice for people looking for an efficient note-taking application.

When it comes to text editing, it is easy to tell that OneNote app is superior mainly because of the rich text formatting features that come with it. These features allow users to organize the text they place on their notebooks appropriately. With Google Keep, it is not possible to do this. Instead of organizing text, pressing the enter button creates new file on Google Keep

Google Keep tends to be a choice for people who want to keep things simple. However, if you are not just looking at simplicity, but want to experience a wide range of ways to get things done completed while exploring different features that enhance your ability to keep notes intact, OneNote is your best choice.

Other Applications Similar to OneNote
EverNote and GoogleKeep are two among other applications that are considered to be very similar to OneNote. However, but there are others that offer similar features. They include the following:

- **CintaNotes:**Just as its name suggests this is an application that allows you to add notes is a very straightforward way. Though this application is pretty simple and easy to use, it does not come with most features that OneNote offers. Compared to OneNote, its features are very basic and limited. Some of the things that you can expect to do with CintaNotes application is tagging snippets of text from various documents that you may have read or received.

- **NeverNote:**This was initially created to run on Linux operating system and isonly after some time that it became available for Windows platforms. While NeverNote serves more as a response to EverNote than OneNote, it is not very functional. Users tend to have a hard time trying to understand how to work with this application.

- **TiddlyWiki:**If you have been looking for apps to enable you organize your documents better, you may have come across this application before finding. While it does much of what OneNote can do, OneNote can still do that those things much better. There are many shortcuts that one has to learn before they can use the TiddlyWiki application with ease compared to OneNote. OneNote does not require users to learn numerous shortcuts to use it, an aspect that makes it distinct from TiddlyWiki

It is clear that there are different applications and software available for note taking running on various platforms. When you compare all these applications, OneNote still emerges as the best choice. This is largely due to the options in terms of features that it offers users that build their confidence in organizing their personal and work related things based on their needs.

Conclusion

OneNote is a great tool for many different kinds of people; students, writers, people who want to organize their notes better and also those that wants to enjoy the flexibility its features provide. It is a very easy to use too that has a lot to offer its user in the end.

It is a program that works best if used together with Word and Outlook, therefore, if you have been using it alone, you may not be getting its full benefits. You can choose to have the free version or the paid version. Note that the latter version has more advanced features that could benefit the user so much.

It is believed that OneNote is only useful for tablet PCs, which is not the case at all. If this was the case, it would mean that only a few people would be benefiting from the features of this software. The truth is OneNote can perform very well in any platform particularly in Windows powered machines. The use of OneNote should not be limited to taking notes and organizing them only. From this eBook, you can clearly see a lot of other things that you can do with it including integrating media files and photos to your notes. As you continue using the program, you will realize that you will achieve a lot from its features.

It is evident that OneNote is something that can be used in various platforms and although the type of things that it can do may vary a bit, it does not change the fact that it is very useful for note - taking. It is something that can be used anytime, anywhere.

I hope this exclusive guide will be of great help to you as a

OneNote user, and that it will help you achieve more using your software. I hope it has helped OneNote users realize some of the things they had not discovered about it.If you haven't tried this application out for one reason or another, I hope this guide has helped you understand the range of benefits you can derive from using OneNote. If you have been contemplating on whether or not you are going to leave your pen and paper soon, you now know that OneNote can help you make the right decision.

FREE BONUS

Just to say thank-you for buying my book, I'd like to offer you **FREE access to OurBookClub.co**

I think you will benefit immensely for joining as you will gain fast access to tons of **FREE EXCLUSIVE CONTENT:**

Signup Bonus (Download):

The Prosperity Bundle (three eBooks):

- ☐ Top 10 Ideas to attract Money
- ☐ Top 10 Ideas to attract Health
- ☐ Top 10 ideas to attract Healthy Relationships

In These 3 FREE BOOKS You'll Learn:

How to build wealth easily, manage your life to attract

good health, enhance your current relationships, and

attract "The One"

Other Benefits for joining OurBookClub:

☐ FREE brand new eBooks (from Gardening, Programming, Cookbooks, Spirituality, Fiction, Self-help and more...)

☐ Be informed of discounted eBooks

☐ Chance to have a say in what content you would like for us to add to new book editions

☐ Free Articles & Videos

☐ Free Access to an active readers community (soon to be launched)

Ready? **Get Access Now**

16424918R00045

Printed in Poland
by Amazon Fulfillment
Poland Sp. z o.o., Wrocław